MY VERY OWN BOOK OF

FLAGS

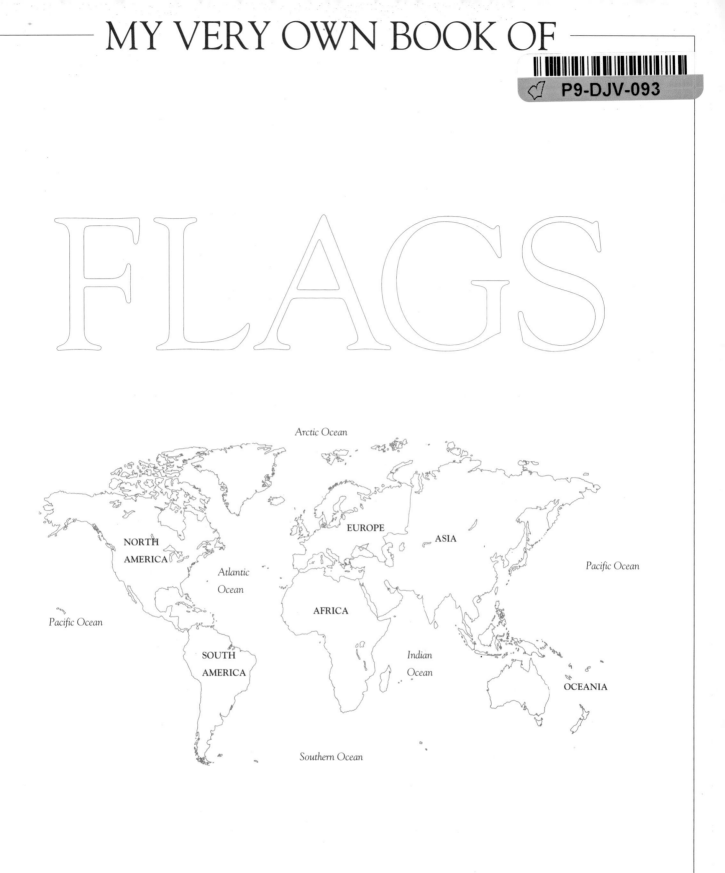

Arctic Ocean

EUROPE ASIA

NORTH
AMERICA

Atlantic
Ocean

Pacific Ocean

Pacific Ocean

AFRICA

SOUTH
AMERICA

Indian
Ocean

OCEANIA

Southern Ocean

Designed by

EUROPE

Iceland

Faeroe Islands
(Denmark)

Atlantic Ocean

Norway

Sweden

North Sea

Denmark

Baltic Sea

Ireland

United Kingdom

Netherlands

Poland

Belgium

Germany

Luxembourg

Czech Republic

Austria

Liechtenstein

Switzerland

Slovenia

Croatia

Italy

Bosnia and
Herzegovina

France

Monaco

San
Marino

Andorra

Mediterranean Sea

Portugal

Spain

ASIA

Finland

Estonia

Russian Federation

Latvia

Lithuania

Belorussia

Caspian Sea

Ukraine

lovakia

Moldavia

Hungary

Black Sea

Romania

Yugoslavia

Bulgaria

Macedonia

Albania

Greece

Turkey

ASIA

EUROPE

Turkey

Georgia

Kazakhstan

Cyprus

Armenia
Azerbaijan

Uzbekistan

Lebanon
Israel

Syria

Turkmenistan

Kyrgyzstan

Jordan

Iraq

Tajikistan

Kuwait

Iran

Saudi
Arabia

Afghanistan

Bahrain

Qatar

United
Arab Emirates

Pakistan

Nepal

Oman

Yemen

India

AFRICA

Indian Ocean

Sri
Lanka

Russian Federation

Pacific Ocean

Mongolia

North
Korea

Japan

South
Korea

China

Taiwan

Bhutan

Macao

Bangladesh

Hong Kong

Philippines

SOUTH-EAST
ASIA

SOUTH-EAST ASIA AND OCEANIA

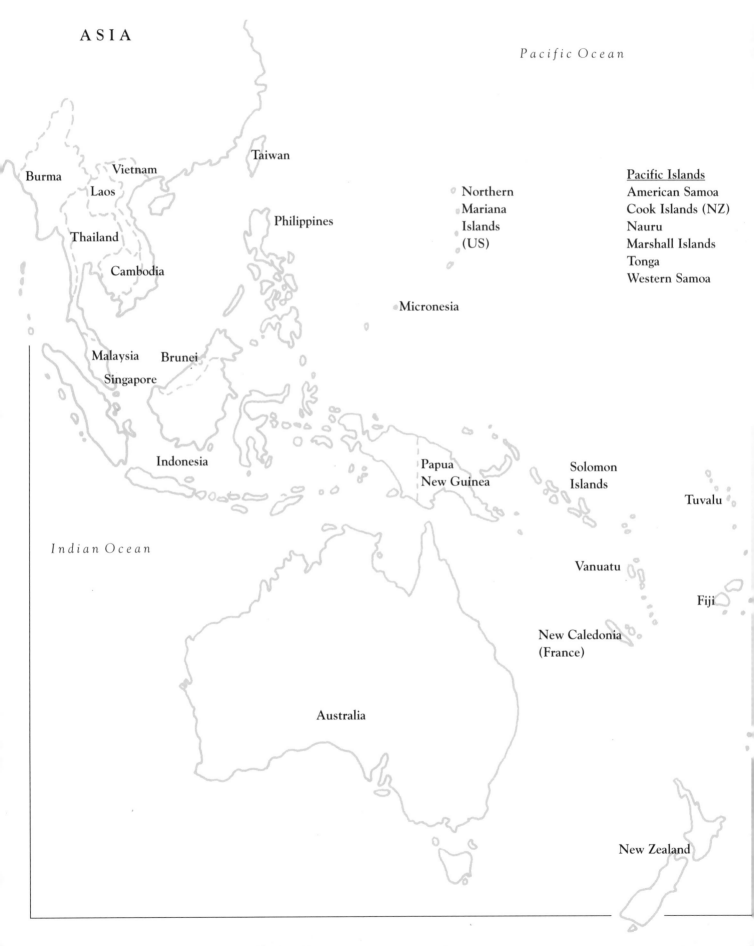

ASIA

Pacific Ocean

Taiwan

Burma

Vietnam

Laos

Thailand

Cambodia

Philippines

Northern
Mariana
Islands
(US)

Pacific Islands
American Samoa
Cook Islands (NZ)
Nauru
Marshall Islands
Tonga
Western Samoa

Micronesia

Malaysia   Brunei

Singapore

Indonesia

Papua
New Guinea

Solomon
Islands

Tuvalu

Indian Ocean

Vanuatu

Fiji

New Caledonia
(France)

Australia

New Zealand

AMERICA

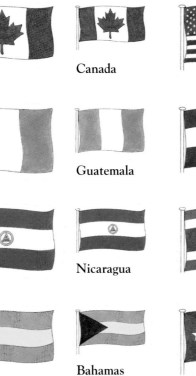 Canada

  USA

  Mexico

Guatemala

El Salvador

 Honduras

Nicaragua

Costa Rica

 Panama

Bahamas

Cuba

Jamaica

Puerto Rico (US)

Barbados

Trinidad and Tobago

Colombia

Venezuela

Guyana

 Surinam

Ecuador

Peru

Bolivia

Brazil

Paraguay

Uruguay

Chile

Argentina

EUROPE

 Iceland

  Norway

 Sweden

 Finland

 Denmark

 United Kingdom

 Ireland

 France

 Spain

 Portugal

 Netherlands

 Belgium

 Luxembourg

 Germany

 Switzerland

 Austria

 Hungary

 Czech Republic

 Poland

 Russian Federation

 Ukraine

 Belorussia

 Italy

 Albania

 Romania

 Bulgaria

 Greece

AFRICA

Morocco
Algeria
Tunisia

Libya
Egypt
Western Sahara

Mauritania
Mali
Burkina

Niger
Chad
Sudan

Ethiopia
Djibouti
Somalia

Senegal
Gambia
Guinea-Bissau

Guinea
Sierra Leone
Liberia

Ivory Coast
Togo
Benin

AFRICA

 Ghana

 Nigeria

 Cameroon

 Central African Republic

 Equatorial Guinea

 Gabon

 Congo

 Congo (Zaire)

 Uganda

 Burundi

 Kenya

 Tanzania

 Angola

 Zambia

 Malawi

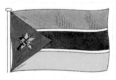 Mozambique

 Namibia

 Botswana

 Swaziland

 Zimbabwe

 Lesotho

 South Africa

 Madagascar

 Mauritius

ASIA

  Turkey

 Syria

  Iraq

Lebanon

 Israel

 Jordan

 Saudi Arabia

Kuwait

Bahrain

Qatar

United Arab
Emirates

 Oman

Yemen

 Iran

Afghanistan

Pakistan

India

Nepal

  Bhutan

Bangladesh

  Sri Lanka

China

  Mongolia

  North Korea

 South Korea

  Japan

 Taiwan

SOUTH-EAST ASIA AND OCEANIA

 Burma

 Thailand

 Laos

 Cambodia

 Vietnam

 Philippines

 Malaysia

 Singapore

 Brunei

 Indonesia

 Australia

 Australian Aboriginal flag

 Papua New Guinea

 Nthn Mariana Islands (US)

 Micronesia

 Marshall Islands

 Solomon Islands

 Nauru

 Fiji

 Western Samoa

 American Samoa

 New Zealand

 Cook Islands (NZ)

 Tonga

NORTH AMERICA

Alaska
(US)

Greenland
(Denmark)

Canada

United States of America

Atlantic Ocean

Pacific Ocean

Mexico

Belize

Caribbean Sea

Guatemala

Honduras

El Salvador

Nicaragua

Costa Rica

Panama

SOUTH
AMERICA

THE CARIBBEAN

Atlantic Ocean

United States of America

Bahamas

Cuba

Turks and Caicos Islands (UK)

Cayman Islands (UK)

Jamaica

Haiti

Dominican Republic

Puerto Rico (US)

Virgin Islands (US/UK)

Anguilla (UK)

Antigua and Barbuda

St Kitts and Nevis

Montserrat (UK)

Guadeloupe (France)

Dominica

Martinique (France)

St Lucia

Caribbean Sea

Aruba (Netherlands)

Netherlands Antilles

St Vincent and the Grenadines

Grenada

Barbados

Trinidad and Tobago

SOUTH AMERICA

SOUTH AMERICA

CENTRAL
AMERICA

Venezuela   Guyana

                         Surinam   French Guiana

Colombia

Ecuador

Peru

Pacific Ocean

Bolivia   Brazil

                    Paraguay

Chile

                                    Atlantic Ocean

            Uruguay

    Argentina

NORTHERN AFRICA

Morocco

Tunisia

Western
Sahara

Algeria

Mauritania

Mali

Senegal

Gambia

Niger

Guinea-
Bissau

Burkina

Guinea

Benin

Sierra
Leone

Togo

Liberia

Nigeria

Ivory Coast

Ghana

Cameroon

Atlantic Ocean

Mediterranean Sea

ASIA

Libya

Egypt

Red Sea

Chad

Eritrea

Djibouti

Sudan

Somalia

Central African Republic

Ethiopia

SOUTHERN AFRICA

Indian Ocean

SOUTHERN AFRICA

NORTHERN AFRICA

Equatorial
Guinea

Gabon

Congo

Congo
(Zaire)

Uganda

Rwanda

Burundi

Kenya

Indian Ocean

Tanzania

Angola

Zambia

Malawi

Mozambique

Zimbabwe

Botswana

Madagascar

Namibia

Swaziland

Lesotho

Atlantic
Ocean

South Africa

A SPECIAL STRENGTH

Written by
Michael Burgan

McGraw Hill

THIS BOOK IS THE PROPERTY OF:

STATE_____

PROVINCE_____

COUNTY_____

PARISH_____

SCHOOL DISTRICT_____

OTHER_____

Book No. _____

Enter information in spaces to the left as instructed

ISSUED TO	Year Used	CONDITION	
		ISSUED	RETURNED

PUPILS to whom this textbook is issued must not write on any page or mark any part of it in any way, consumable textbooks excepted.

1. Teachers should see that the pupil's name is clearly written in ink in the spaces above in every book issued.
2. The following terms should be used in recording the condition of the book: New; Good; Fair; Poor; Bad.

McGraw-Hill School Division

A Division of The McGraw-Hill Companies

McGraw-Hill School Division
1221 Avenue of the Americas
New York, New York 10020

Book Design and Production: Kirchoff/Wohlberg, Inc.

Printed in the United States of America

ISBN 0-02-147795-7

3 4 5 6 7 8 9 066 03 02 01 00 99

A SPECIAL STRENGTH

Written by
Michael Burgan

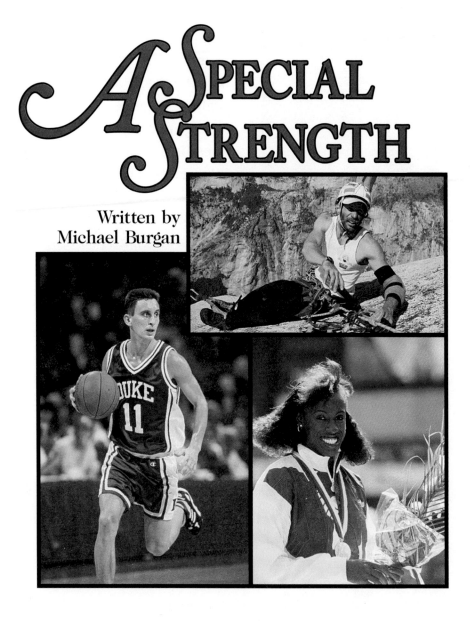

**Macmillan
McGraw-Hill**

New York   Farmington

What does it take to be a champion?

The best baseball pitchers throw the ball over and over on the sidelines. They train to strengthen their arms and perfect their windups.

In gymnastics, kids barely old enough to go to school practice every day. After years of running, jumping, and building their bodies, a few are good enough to compete around the world.

In every sport, from archery to wrestling, athletes work hard to reach their goals. They have a single focus: being the best they can be. But some champion athletes have a special strength. This strength has nothing to do with lifting weights or knocking down opponents. It's an inner strength—inside these athletes' minds and hearts.

An accident or illness might make some people give up a sport or feel sorry for themselves. But for the three athletes you're about to meet, their inner strength has helped them beat their physical problems. Nothing stops a true champion.

2

Bobby's Battle

Bobby Hurley's limp body lay in the mud. His face sat in a small pool of water. Just moments before, a car had rammed Bobby's truck on a California road. The collision sent the truck flying 127 feet through the air. Hurley, who was not wearing a seat belt, was tossed out of the truck.

Pain shot through Bobby's body. Some people who drove by the accident stopped to help him. Bobby wanted to know just one thing: "Am I going to die?"

A few hours before the accident, Hurley had been playing basketball for the Sacramento Kings. Hurley was a rookie. He was small for a pro basketball player–just 6 feet tall. But from the first time he stepped on a court, Bobby played hard. He played to win.

Bobby grew up in Jersey City, New Jersey. In seventh grade, when he was still under five feet tall, Bobby played with high school players. When he reached high school, Bobby led his team to four state championships. The team lost only five games in those four years.

In college, Bobby helped the Duke Blue Devils win two national championships. One sportswriter called Bobby the best college basketball player in the country. After his senior year at Duke, Bobby joined the National Basketball Association and began earning millions of dollars.

Now, the rookie was lying in the mud. And he probably was going to die. At a local hospital, the doctors who examined Bobby found many injuries. He had two crushed lungs, broken ribs, and other broken bones. Some of his muscles were torn. A deep cut ran from his left eye to his ear.

Worst of all, Bobby's windpipe had separated from one of his lungs. Normally, air enters the body through the mouth or nose, then goes through the windpipe to the lungs. Usually, when the windpipe separates from a lung, a patient dies. The doctors thought Bobby would be lucky to live a week.

Lying in his hospital bed, Bobby coughed up blood. Air leaked out of his damaged lungs and his body blew up like a balloon. Bobby had an operation so the doctors could repair his broken bones and damaged lungs. Afterward, Bobby's whole body ached so much, it was hard to get out of bed. But an amazing thing happened: In less than two weeks, Bobby Hurley was ready to leave the hospital.

Bobby had fought for his life and won. Now he had another fight ahead: playing basketball again. Bobby went home to New Jersey to begin his training. A few months after the accident, he ran for the first time. He lifted weights and did 500 sit-ups a day. By April 1994, Bobby was once again dribbling a ball and driving to the basket.

At first, Bobby says, his body couldn't catch up with what his mind wanted to do. He played against high school and college players, trying to relearn his old skills. Finally, when the 1994-95 NBA season began, Bobby was ready to play.

Bobby once again played guard for the Sacramento Kings. He averaged 4.2 points and 3.3 assists per game. His performance wasn't as good as it had been back in college, but Bobby was still learning how to play the pro game. And with a healthy body, he would have plenty of time to improve.

Bobby may never play on another championship team or win any awards, but he's still happy. After all he's been through, Bobby says, "just playing basketball again is like a reward."

The Greatest Ever

Her muscular arms and legs pump up and down as Jackie Joyner-Kersee speeds around the track.

Picking up the shot put, a heavy metal ball, Jackie heaves it almost fifty feet.

After a fast sprint, Jackie leaps into the air and soars for more than 24 feet. When she lands in the sand pit, Jackie smiles a winner's grin.

Jackie Joyner-Kersee has been called the world's greatest female athlete ever. Some sports experts say she might be America's best athlete, man or woman. Jackie has been a track-and-field star since 1984, when she won her first Olympic medal.

But many sports fans don't know that when Jackie runs and jumps and throws, she is always in danger of getting sick. Jackie has asthma, an illness that makes it hard for a person to breathe. But Jackie won't let her asthma stop her. All her life, Jackie has fought hard to beat any problem that got in her way.

When she was nine, Jackie became interested in sports. She had long legs and was a fast runner, so she decided to enter a track meet. In her first race, she came in last. That poor finish didn't discourage Jackie. It only pushed her to try harder.

With years of training, Jackie grew stronger and faster. By the time she went to college, she was a great runner and basketball player. Bob Kersee, a track coach at the school, saw that Jackie could be an even better track athlete. He began to prepare Jackie for the heptathlon. The heptathlon is a two-day competition featuring seven running, throwing, and jumping events.

Jackie's training went well. But one day, Jackie had to stop running. She bent over at the waist and gasped for air. Something was wrong.

Jackie soon felt better. But the frightening feeling of not being able to breathe happened again and again.

Finally, Jackie went to a doctor. The doctor told her she had asthma. A lot of things can cause asthma: air pollution, stress, allergies. But Jackie's asthma was caused by exercise. The thing she loved most was making her sick.

After that, Jackie rested whenever she felt an attack starting. She also took medicine. Nothing was going to stop her from being the best she could be.

And Jackie's best was awesome. At the 1984 Summer Olympics, she just missed winning the gold medal in the heptathlon. In 1986, Jackie set two world records and was named the best amateur athlete in the United States. Then, at the 1988 Summer Olympics, Jackie won gold medals in the heptathlon and the long jump.

Jackie seemed to have her asthma under control. But after the 1988 Olympics, she had her worst attack ever. She began coughing and couldn't stop. Bob Kersee, now her husband, rushed her to the hospital. During the next year, Jackie's asthma began to bother her more often. But she wouldn't stop training or competing.

As an international track athlete, Jackie faced a special problem. Most people with asthma can take the strongest medicines available to fight their illness. But track athletes can't use certain medicines while they're competing. These medicines can speed up the body, which can help an athlete run faster or jump farther than usual. After taking one asthma drug, Jackie would have to stop competing for a few weeks.

As she's gotten older, Jackie's asthma has gotten worse.
Sometimes she practices with an inhaler in her pocket. The
inhaler gives her medicine if she has a sudden attack. In 1994,
Jackie twice had attacks while she was running in meets. She
was able to finish her races, but her lungs burned and she fought
for air as she ran.

All athletes get hurt from time to time. They pull muscles or
twist ankles. Jackie's had her share of those injuries, too. But
those kinds of injuries eventually get better. Jackie's asthma will
never go away. She never knows when she'll feel that burning in
her chest. But she's never let it slow her down. "I have learned,"
she says, "to push myself up and get on with my life."

No Barriers

Mark Wellman made his way down the mountain. He had just finished climbing the Seven Gables, in California's Sierra Nevadas. Wellman had been climbing mountains since he was twelve. For him, it was as easy as riding a bike or tossing ball.

Suddenly, Mark's foot slipped on some crumbled rocks. He tumbled down the mountain, falling 100 feet. When he landed, he couldn't move. His back was broken.

On that day in the Sierra Nevadas, Mark Wellman became physically disabled. After the fall, Mark was a paraplegic–he would never be able to use his legs again. Most paraplegics spend their lives in wheelchairs. But Mark was determined to keep climbing mountains and living an active life.

Mark had many battles to fight before he could return to the mountains. First, he had to find a positive attitude again. Mark's injuries depressed him. It was hard for a strong, energetic young man to accept the fact that he'd never walk again. Mark also had to learn new ways to climb and do the other sports he loved. From now on, he'd only be able use the strength in his arms.

Mark worked hard to get his body in shape. He played tennis while sitting in a wheelchair. He swam for hours in a pool. And he lifted weights to make his arms even stronger than they were before. Finally, Mark was ready for his first major climb since the accident.

In 1989, Mark and his new climbing partner, Mike Corbett, set out to climb the face of El Capitan. El Capitan soars almost 3,000 feet above Yosemite National Park. It's the highest granite rock in the world. El Capitan has a flat surface, like a wall in a room. Mark became the first paraplegic climber to reach the top of El Capitan.

Mark has kept on climbing since he scaled El Capitan. He's also become active in other sports. Before his accident, Mark was a downhill skier, and he still loves to speed down the slopes. Now, he also skies cross country. He took part in the 1992 and 1994 Winter Para-Olympics, an event where paraplegics and other physically challenged athletes from around the world compete for medals.

To make cross-country skiing easier, Mark created new equipment for paraplegics. Paraplegic skiers sit on a small seat attached to one ski. Mark improved this design. In 1993, he took his sit-ski on a 50-mile trek across the Sierra Nevadas, skiing trails 10,000 feet high.

Mark has shown that paraplegics can conquer more than mountains–they can ride the waves, too. Inside a kayak (a kind of canoe), Mark rushes down whitewater rivers. For a more leisurely ride, Mark sometimes takes his kayak to the Pacific Ocean. There, he paddles near the whales that play along the California coast.

After Mark Wellman fell that day on the Seven Gables, he could have given up the sports he loves. Instead, he found the inner strength to meet the challenge of his disability. He refused to let his disability become a barrier–something that stopped him from moving forward.

Today, Mark believes people can do anything they want to, if they try hard enough. Mark travels the country, sharing that message with both the physically challenged and the physically able.

The wilderness that Mark loves made him a paraplegic. But he says it gave him something, too: a life full of challenge and joy. Mark adds, "Everyone faces the world with different abilities and disabilities. But everyone has at least one goal in common–to break through their own barriers."